LISTEN
TO THE
HUNGER

LISTEN
TO THE
HUNGER

WHY WE OVEREAT

ELISABETH L.

HARPER/HAZELDEN

First Harper & Row edition published in 1988.

ISBN 0-06-255469-7
LC 87-45706

89   90   91   92   MPC   10   9   8   7   6   5   4   3

CONTENTS

INTRODUCTION

If someone habitually overeats, it is safe to say that person is hooked on using food to do things food cannot do. Habitual overeating is an addiction as powerful as the addiction to alcohol or other drugs. In many ways, it is even more difficult to deal with food abuse, since no one can stop eating completely. We can put alcohol and other drugs out of our lives. We do not need either substance for survival. We do need food. We must find a way to identify our legitimate hunger for food without letting it expand and absorb other hungers that need to be fed.

If, whenever we feel a twinge of emotion, our first impulse is to put something in our mouths, we are misreading our inner signals. The key to getting "unstuck" is learning to pay attention to what is behind the craving for excess food. What needs are being masked or covered up by the desire to eat more? What is the hunger about?

The path away from food abuse leads out of the boredom and despair of compulsion into a many-splendored world of feeling and participation. The way out is sometimes steep and twisting, with temporary roadblocks, detours, and slippery places. It is a path to be traveled daily with all the aid and assistance we can get. Professional healers can help. So can fellow travelers, especially those who are working a Twelve Step program. Our greatest resource — which is always available — is the inner voice that tells us who we are, what we feel, and what we need. If we will take time to listen and learn, we will slowly discover what the hunger is all about. The hunger will lead to an ever-increasing knowledge of what life is all about. We will grow through our hungers into greater understanding and strength. Each day will be richer and fuller. We will not cease to be hungry, but we will learn what satisfies.

We need to rely on a Power greater than ourselves, but food is not that Power.

ONE

Won't Somebody Please
Take Care of Me?

Scratch beneath the surface of an eating disorder and before you go very far you will come to a layer of dependency. I may think I'm the very soul of independence — I live by myself, support myself, even take myself to dinner and the movies when there's no one to go with. But if I'm so independent, why is it that I want to head for the refrigerator when I return to an empty house? Why do I crave three bowls of cereal and two peanut butter sandwiches when breakfast, lunch, and dinner were entirely adequate?

In the beginning we were nourished in a nice, warm womb. We emerged, the cord was cut, we cried when we were hungry, and someone — usually a mother — fed us. We were helpless, and someone took care of us, or we wouldn't be here today. After a couple of years, we were less helpless. We could feed ourselves if someone gave us the food and utensils. Then we went to school and ate in a cafeteria where we may have had to take what was served. At home, we became increasingly proficient at choosing and consuming meals and maybe snacks. By the time we were on our own, most of us were quite capable of taking care of our nutritional needs, either through buying and preparing food, eating out, or a combination of both.

While all of this body feeding was going on, what else was happening? We were getting emotional messages as well as physical nourishment. If we were lucky, there was warmth, tenderness, approval, and fun, as well as calories. Most likely from time to time, there was also some anger, hostility, and anxiety during meals. What was consistent, as long as one or more people were present with us while we were eating, was a sense of *connectedness*. Even if we ate with a caretaker who sat with us in stony silence, someone was there. We were not alone.

There may have been times when we did eat alone. Perhaps your mother gave you a bottle when she put you to bed for the night. Maybe you had some solitary suppers on a tray in front of the television set. Even so, the experience of eating evoked the association of being fed by someone else before you were big enough to hold your own bottle and spoon. Since our early nourishment had to come by way of another human being, eating is still etched somewhere in our awareness as a time when we were cared for. Being fed meant being taken care of.

The connection is still there. Food means, if not love, at least interrelatedness. For the time while I am eating, I am not alone in a cold, cruel world. There is the memory, conscious or unconscious, of someone nearby who is looking after me and my needs. I feel relatively secure, if only for the moment. And so, I like to eat. When did I start eating more for emotional comfort and support than for bodily need? Were the two ever separate? How did the emotional factor so eclipse the physical one that I could overeat to the point of damaging my body?

I may never come up with answers to those questions. For now, what I need to do is become more aware of my dependency needs. When I am hungry at an inappropriate time — for example, one hour after a complete dinner — I can try to feel down through the surface of the hunger into my "independent" dependence. I may never reach completely through it, but I can make a start.

I am a single woman. I grew up during a time when a girl was expected to become a wife and a mother, to be provided for by the man who was her husband and the father of her children. I dreamed of the knight in shining armor who would carry me off on his white horse to live in a land of perpetual bliss. At the age of twenty-three, I left my hometown in a black Volkswagon convertible with my new husband whose naval uniform was to me a reasonable facsimile of shining armor. For the next twenty-three years, there were not many discouraging words — not spoken ones. When something was wrong, I was more likely to overeat than talk about it. There was some bliss, but there was a lot of dependency.

I certainly thought I was in love with the man I married. The fact that I wasn't thrilled with the job I had when I met him, and the fact that I had very little confidence in my ability to take care of myself, did not become apparent to me until many years later. I was certainly looking for romance. Was I also looking for someone to take care of me?

I continued to work during the first year of the marriage until getting pregnant rescued me from teaching at a school for girls. I was dismayed at the prospect of becoming a mother — how could I take care of someone else when I couldn't make it on my own? But, after all, that was what you did when you got married. You had children.

We had two. Miraculously, as they grew, I grew. Unfortunately, the marriage deteriorated. Too many binges, too many cocktail hours, and not enough communication. Love on the rocks. When my youngest child was eighteen, I pushed myself out of the nest to try to fly on my own. Interestingly enough, at least one eye would wander around still looking for someone to take care of me.

Women are more prone to developing eating disorders than men. Women traditionally have had the more dependent role, at least on the surface. Have men been equally or more dependent emotionally? Does the higher incidence of

7

alcoholism among men indicate the same dependency has manifested itself in different ways? (The current increase in alcohol abuse among women seems to be eradicating that difference.)

We are all dependent. It's part of the human condition. The question is, do we recognize our dependency and do we choose to lean on something strong enough to give us the support we need? Cereal and peanut butter sandwiches, especially when consumed in binge-style proportions, simply will not do the job. Neither will Scotch and soda. People do better, but they're not always around in the right size and shape and mood.

We pay a high price for our dependencies when they turn out to make us weaker instead of stronger. We can sell our souls to ice cream or to alcohol or to the corporation or to the wrong relationship. None of these will take care of us unconditionally forever. Not even the right relationship will do that.

Shredded wheat is not a very good substitute for Mother, but when Mother is no longer available we may try to replace her with food. In the process of growing up, girls have to do more than grow away from their dependence on Mother. They usually become mothers themselves. They move away from being nurtured into doing the nurturing.

And who mothers the mothers? We can continue to receive nurturing. It may come from a variety of sources — other women, the men who love us, our children, people in the helping professions. If, however, the nurturing we need doesn't come to us automatically, and if we don't know how to ask for it, or if we're too proud to admit we need it, then we may get hung up on substitutes like too much food or too much alcohol or too many pills.

The hunger is there. Something inside us still wants Mommy when the going gets rough, or even when something wonderful has happened which we want to share. For most of us, Mommy or her substitute was there for us at least part of the time. If we seldom or never had a mother figure, the hunger is more acute and more difficult to identify.

If we have grown up without making new linkages with people who can satisfy our ongoing needs for support and nurturing, we may put substances in their place. For me, something sweet was very early a source of comfort and pleasure. When I had to take milk of magnesia, my mother would give me a marshmallow afterwards to make the bad taste go away. I saved candy to have when I wanted comfort. The pleasure of one piece of candy eventually became the pain of a half-gallon of ice cream.

Since we are originally dependent on parents for our physical and emotional survival, their approval is of supreme importance. "Mommy's good girl" eats what she is supposed to when she is supposed to, often without much regard for inner cues and signals. Eating gets tied into receiving approval as well as nourishment. If I don't eat the way I'm supposed to, Mommy and Daddy will not like me, and then what will I do? I can't get food for myself, so I will die without their care. Emotionally, I will die without their love and approval.

Mommy and Daddy never told me to eat a half-gallon of ice cream. That was my idea. It was a progressive decision. When one dish didn't quite give me that wonderful feeling of all's right with my world (although I had finished my meat and vegetables before eating the ice cream), perhaps another dish would do the trick.

If it was a dark afternoon and I was home alone and I was supposed to be practicing the piano but the piece was hard to play, would a sliver of cake help in the same way that the marshmallow had helped? A sliver worked at the beginning but, after a few years, half of the cake would disappear.

It was as if I thought I might be able to face the world alone only if I had a stash of sugar to support me. One day my parents would be dead, and then I would truly be on my own. It was a terrifying thought, but somehow more endurable on a full stomach. While I was eating, I could push the frightening thought away and revel in the soft sweetness that told me everything was okay in my world.

Many years and many cavities later, I realized that sugar had to go, along with alcohol, which had become part of my support system ever since I was twenty-one. Sugar had been a friend for at least twenty-eight years and alcohol for eighteen. After the initial pain of parting company with them, I felt a lot better, but dependency was still making me hungry.

That's when I switched to foods like shredded wheat and cheese for binges. They kept my blood sugar level on a more even keel, but they were still binge foods, consumed in large quantities between meals. Instead of confronting the hunger and learning from it, I was resorting to a pseudosolution.

Mothers and fathers will not be with us forever. Lovers can turn fickle and leave, or become sullen and withdrawn. Children have their own lives to live, and friends may be out of town when we need them. Where do we find the support we crave? We need people we can count on, and the time and energy we put into cultivating deep relationships can reap a rich harvest. For some of us these relationships may seem to be enough, but others of us are still hungry.

According to the Big Book of Alcoholics Anonymous,

> . . . deep down in every man, woman, and child, is the fundamental idea of God. It may be obscured by calamity, by pomp, by worship of other things, but in some form or other it is there. For faith in a Power greater than ourselves, and miraculous demonstrations of that power in human lives, are facts as old as man himself.[1]

Could it be we each have a special, inner hunger which all the nutritious food and human companionship in the world will not satisfy? Could it be we are intended to be spiritually dependent on a Power greater than ourselves, as well as physically dependent on the elements of our environment and emotionally dependent on the people close to us?

How do we get it all together without falling into the trap of false dependencies such as food or substance abuse, or harmful relationships, or the spiritual pride which seduces us with the idea of going it alone until self-will runs riot?

Listening to the inner voice is crucial. It is the key to unlocking our true needs and separating them from false dependencies. To listen, we must take time away from our busy schedules and get to know our inner selves. How do I know I want my mother's support, love, and encouragement instead of shredded wheat? I need to take time to listen to the child inside of me before drowning out the voice of that child with more food than my body requires. I may be able to nurture my inner child by myself or I may need help from someone else. But I can't do either until I take time to hear what the child is saying and feel what the child is feeling.

Could it be that my spiritual self is a child hungry for the love and support of a Higher Power? Is it possible this spiritual part of me needs daily nourishment to keep my life integrated and on track? Is my hunger for more food, more mother's love, and more approval really a sign that I am spiritually undernourished?

Who is going to take care of me? I'd like to be able to do it all by myself so I wouldn't be dependent on anyone else. So far, I have not succeeded. Underneath my independent dependence is a ravenous child who grabs on to the idea of unlimited food, sex, money, and various other things as solutions to the emptiness. This hungry child is misguided, since the solutions don't work.

If I can't take care of myself, and if excess quantities of the things I like don't magically make me feel secure, and if I haven't been able to recruit a satisfactory human caretaker, what am I going to do?

As I think about it, I realize for nearly half a century I have had care. The perception that I am alone and independent in a dangerous and hostile world is a distorted one. I have had care from parents, teachers, friends, lovers, children, therapists, myself, you, and everyone else who helps to keep our society functioning. We are not separate. We are all a part of each other.

We may feel alone. We may feel we need support. We do need support, but we are not alone. We have support and it's more than food. It's talking to a friend and listening. It's the Higher Power that speaks through our friends and through our inner voice. We may not have mothers or fathers to take care of us now, and we don't want to turn the people who are close to us into parents, but care is available. It's all around as we reach out for advice from a co-worker, information from the library, help from a physician, love from family and friends. It comes to us and we give it back and everyone has more to share.

The faith that we are cared for even when we don't quite understand what's going on is a gift. We get ready to receive the gift by giving up our misguided sense of independence and opening ourselves to the care that surrounds us. It does not come from just one person but from many. When we acknowledge a Higher Power is in charge of our lives, we can trust we will receive what we need when we need it.

My hunger to be cared for is a basic one and will be with me as long as I live. If I don't take it seriously, I can be sidetracked into harmful dependencies. When I listen to this need and seek a positive way of filling it, I eventually come to a Higher Power, whom I choose to call God. If I would come to this Higher Power sooner rather than later, I would avoid much pain and grief. When I make contact with my center, I have the feeling that all is right with my world since for that moment I know I am in the heart of God.

When we were babies, being fed brought the safety of our mothers' arms. As adults, we subconsciously give food a sort of magic ability to ward off real or imagined danger.

TWO

Running Scared

When I was six I was afraid of dogs and afraid I would never learn how to read. I was probably afraid of many more things, but those are the fears I remember most vividly today.

I didn't have a dog myself, but there was a black one next door who terrified me. Usually he was in a fenced backyard, but every so often he got out. He barked at me and chased me, and I ran to the safety of the side porch. I wouldn't go out again until my mother had called the owner and the dog was back inside the fence.

I did learn to read when I was six, but I never thought it would happen. I loved books. As an only child of parents who were both teachers, I was read to often and enthusiastically. I don't know why I was afraid I wouldn't be able to do it myself, but I do know the idea of learning to read filled me with great anxiety and also with anticipation. Why did I think I couldn't do it? Why was I scared?

When I was sixteen I was afraid of sex and afraid of playing the piano in public. Some of my fear of sex had to do with my fear of getting pregnant. I was afraid of playing the piano in public because I was afraid of making mistakes or, even worse, forgetting the music.

Eventually I got over my surface fear of sex, although a deeper fear of complete surrender and vulnerability still lingers. Playing the piano in public is something I gave up on long ago, but I still have occasional nightmares about being

15

on stage and forgetting the music. I'm often scared now that my job performance won't be good enough. And I'm scared to ride on a motorcycle or dive off a high diving board. The last two activities I can avoid, but I need to hold down a job in order to pay the mortgage and buy groceries.

When I was eleven and scared about my first big piano recital, I would stop practicing and go in search of something sweet to eat. When I was studying for an exam or writing a paper in college, I did the same thing. A couple of cookies became a couple of boxes and more. I ate so much that my stomach was painfully distended. Then I would take laxatives or an enema or fast for a couple of days. If I hadn't had such a horror of vomiting, I would have tried that.

The food didn't work. Fear grew into panic. The panic kept me awake at night. I got anxiety attacks in crowded places. I ran from one college to another and another and back to the first. I finally graduated, panicking through the entire ceremony that I would either faint or throw up.

Fortunately I didn't do either. I picked up my diploma, spent the summer having a hot romance and playing the organ at a country church (where I wasn't too scared because I had the music in front of me). Then I went off to my first real job where, alone in my room in the faculty living quarters, I ate bread by the loaf and cookies by the box after having had dinner in the dining hall.

If I had had more courage, I think I would have tried for a job with a publishing firm instead of teaching music. Bingeing saps courage. Like alcohol for the alcoholic, too much food for the overeater "borrows from the future and it ultimately destroys."[1] Within three months, I was engaged to a young man whom I had known for ten days and had seen six times. Was I afraid of getting married? Yes, but I was more afraid of confronting the fact that I probably would not make it as a musician, in spite of the considerable financial and emotional investment my parents had made in my musical career.

16

Why didn't I have the courage to opt out of recitals years before and get some solid training in another field? My response to the nagging inner fear of failure was to eat. Food was my tranquilizer, along with prescription drugs (Miltown and, later, Doriden) given to me by my family doctor for my "college nerves."

It's okay to be afraid, but I didn't know that until years later. What's not okay is to try to smother the fear with pills, or alcohol, or excess food, or marriage vows, or compulsive work, or a combination. I spent years running scared. I did such a good job of fooling everyone with my confident exterior that I almost fooled myself as well. Inside, it was not a happy tune. It was sheer terror.

When, finally, there were no more places to run with my fears, except to the Twelve Step programs, I sat down and read the Big Book[2] and discovered how egocentric my fears were. I was full of the self-centered fear that I either would not get what I wanted or would lose something that I had. My ambitions were so grandiose. If I couldn't be a star-studded concert pianist, I was a failure. The best is the enemy of the good.

If we bury our fears under our hunger to excel, to be powerful and perfect, the fears get bigger and bigger. The fear that we won't be the *Best* is a healthy one — no one is perpetually best. In this case, a nagging fear is on the side of sanity. It leads us away from the dangerous pride that goes before a fall and guides us into a more realistic assessment of our capabilities.

The question is, can we accept and live with a realistic appraisal of ourselves? Is our self-esteem dependent on being able to achieve brilliant displays of virtuosity in a chosen field of endeavor? What kind of a fantasy have we woven in our minds? There are plenty of opportunities for useful service in this world that don't require superior ability or outstanding intelligence or amazing performances.

Perhaps our ultimate fear is the fear of death: loss of control carried to the extreme. Maybe if we begin to face this fear we can better come to terms with the more minor terrors. If you are in a Twelve Step program and have taken Step Three, you have made a significant beginning in the management of fear. Whether we're talking about the fear of death or the fear of starting a new job, the conviction that God is in charge helps immeasurably.

Using food to deal with fear not only doesn't work but also prevents us from changing the things we can change. We can't change the fact that we will die eventually, but we can change careers. Overeating drains our energy, and we spin our wheels in frustration or give up, rather than moving steadily forward with the realities of our situation.

I can remember being afraid that what I was preparing to serve at a dinner party would not be delicious enough to dazzle my guests. I kept tasting the food until I was convinced my guests would not like the party, the food, or me. Then I went on to eat more of whatever I could find in the kitchen until I had ruined the party for myself. I did this more than once.

For me, the fear of not being good enough, of not being accepted, goes way back. Trying to untangle it may be less productive than stopping the behavior which fuels the feelings of inadequacy. Similar to an alcoholic, the overeater eats to allay fear, and the more he or she eats, the greater the fear becomes. I'm scared, therefore I overeat. I overeat, therefore I'm scared.

Running scared. This is what often happens when we adopt someone else's idea of what we are supposed to be and do. We lose our sense of self, and that's terrifying. If we are trying to please a parent, a spouse, or our peer group rather than to operate out of inner motivation, we will be afraid. We will be cut off from our own internal base of operations. If our sense of self-worth depends on someone else's evaluation and approval, we will never be sure that we are okay.

The external demands loom large. We fear we cannot meet them. Anxiety does strange things to us and makes us very uncomfortable. We may experience physical symptoms such as shortness of breath, chest pains, backaches, insomnia, and other unpleasant effects. Sometimes we interpret feelings of anxiety as hunger pangs. As overeaters we try to soothe ourselves with food. Afraid to face our fears, we eat to try to make them go away, but they get bigger.

Running scared. It also happens when we set our own internal expectations too high. All that our Higher Power expects of us is to be who we are and do what we can. When we seek guidance through prayer and meditation, we are building our inner assurance that whatever the outcome, our efforts are supported. We aren't expected to be perfect. We will make mistakes and fall short of perfection, but we will not be abandoned.

Leaving the results to God builds faith instead of fear. Whatever the outcome, we can accept it by working Step Eleven and praying for the power to live by God's will. In my experience, sincerely praying for just that has quieted many middle-of-the-night terrors. That prayer takes away my fear of failure and shifts my focus from self-will to God's will.

The longer I work my Twelve Step program, the less time I spend running scared, and the more faith and confidence I have. When I came into the program ten years ago, I was hiding from life. I spent a lot of time at home in the kitchen — eating. Working the Steps got me out of the house into a series of more interesting and challenging jobs. Even more important, I began to form closer, more meaningful relationships with other people. Each day I learn more about accepting myself as well as my family and friends.

Comparing myself with others is a sure way of generating fear. Other people invariably appear to be smarter, more together, more competent, more attractive than me. I am afraid I won't measure up, and the fear makes me hungry.

When I listen to my hunger, it tells me I want to be and have all of the things these other people appear to be and have. When I listen more closely, my hunger tells me I want to be accepted. That acceptance first has to come from myself. If I am comfortable with myself, other people will be comfortable with me, and I won't have to overeat in the attempt to overcome my insecurity.

It has been much easier for me to accept myself since coming into closer contact with a Higher Power through the program. A large part of my earlier fear stemmed from being out of touch with God and myself. I was running scared. The farther I traveled away from my center, the more frightening life seemed. The fear served a purpose, since it kept me running in search of what was missing.

For a long time, I searched in the wrong places. I thought I needed achievement and money, and I used food as the nearest available substitute. The fact that the answer to what I was frantically seeking on the outside was *inside* escaped me for a long time. I had to exhaust all of the external possibilities before I was ready to surrender and listen to my inner voice.

When panic strikes, the most difficult thing for me to do is sit still and listen, but that's what will help. I don't have to be afraid of myself anymore, or afraid of life. I also don't have to look too far ahead; God takes care of me one day at a time. I honestly believe that what happens to me each moment is part of God's plan. That's wonderfully reassuring. I may not like what a particular moment brings, but I don't have to get scared and run away. There's no place to go. I'm already here, and here is where I need to be right now.

When we hang on to resentment, we poison ourselves.

THREE

Sweet Revenge

Have you ever binged because you were mad at someone? Was the bingeing an attempt to get even? Did you ever think, "I'll show you!" and then proceed to eat as much junk food as you could find? When the binge was finally over, toward whom did you feel more anger — the other person or yourself? Chances are, by the time you stopped eating, you were more upset with yourself for bingeing than you were with the other person.

Revenge has a way of turning inward. Our negative feelings toward someone else end up being more toxic to ourselves than to the other person. As overeaters, we can't afford to indulge in anger and resentment. Whatever momentary satisfaction we may derive from allowing these feelings free rein is soon dissolved when the net result is a binge.

When I was about ten, I had a friend who had everything, or so it seemed to me. She lived in a very big house with a swimming pool. She had her own horses, and she went to school in a chauffeur-driven Cadillac. She was smart and pretty. She had naturally curly hair and lots of friends. When I visited her at her house, everything seemed so much bigger and better than when she visited me at my house, except for one thing. The food was better at my house — especially the desserts.

Once when my friend and I were having dinner at my house, the dessert was pumpkin chiffon pie with whipped cream and honey on top. My friend was too full to eat more

23

than a bite or two of the pie, but I polished off my large piece with gusto, thinking that if I didn't have horses and a swimming pool, at least I had pumpkin pie.

For decades, something sweet was my consolation and my revenge for many real or imagined deprivations. While eating, I fantasized about being richer, prettier, more popular, more powerful, having what I thought I lacked, doing what I thought I wanted to do. When my long-time boyfriend dumped me for someone else, I had regular revenge binges for years afterwards. Each time, the sweet revenge would turn sour, and each time I would do it again a few days or a few weeks later. I never got even. I only got fat and depressed.

"Don't get mad — get even." Neither works for me. Getting mad destroys my serenity and invites problems with food. Getting even is impossible, since nothing I have or do now will erase the real or imagined hurts of the past. I cannot compensate, but I can voluntarily let go of past hurts so that I can respond freely to the present and live now, instead of being controlled and eventually destroyed by old resentments.

"Living well is the best revenge." This works better, especially when I change *well* to *abstinent*. (By abstinent, I mean eating three meals a day and not bingeing.) For me, living abstinent is the best revenge, if I think I need revenge, but even better is being able to give up the idea of revenge entirely. I can turn over the entire revenge department of my life to my Higher Power, along with everything else.

Turning over specific resentments helps me tremendously. I am often unaware that something is festering until I find myself eating and fantasizing about getting even (or somehow defeating the person whom I feel has slighted me in some way). Listen to the hunger. Why do I want something to eat? Is it because my friend didn't call when he said he would? Is it because I didn't get invited to a particular party? Do I feel put down by a boss or co-worker?

24

Anger builds, especially when we don't express it in a reasonable way when we first feel it. A small anger unexpressed can develop into a huge rage which eventually explodes out of all proportion to the situation. Then we feel guilty for overreacting and being unreasonable.

Overeating is not a good way of getting rid of anger. We may chase the angry feelings away temporarily, but they usually return with greater strength and destructive power. Often the angry feelings turn in on ourselves because we have overeaten — again!

I may start out overeating for revenge, but I end up feeling inadequate. I have lost my abstinence, which is my most valuable possession, since without it everything else that is meaningful in my life is threatened. When food takes control of my life, I feel inferior and helpless. I am the person who suffers from the sweet revenge.

Am I punishing myself? Do I sometimes have a lurking sense that things are going too well? Does part of me need to spoil it so I can get back to the more familiar feeling of being mad at myself? Do I fear the good feelings won't last because they never have before?

The part of me that is adult knows there will always be ups and downs. The highs won't last forever, but neither will the lows. When I am in touch with my center, the swings are less extreme. I don't expect myself to be perfect, and I don't pretend to be all-powerful. Therefore, I don't need to get angry at myself when I make mistakes, nor do I need to harbor resentments toward those who may seem better than me.

"My insides looked at your outsides, and so I drank." If that is true for alcoholics, the same may be said of overeaters, substituting the word "overate" for "drank." My insides looked at your outsides, and so I overate. You seemed so much more together than me. You seemed to have it all, and I resented that. I thought somehow I could compensate with food, but I came out feeling even more inferior.

25

When I labeled sugar and alcohol as hazardous to my health and decided to avoid them, my bouts of revenge were no longer sweet, but I could still get "drunk" on large quantities of healthy foods such as whole wheat bread and butter. Overeating is overeating, no matter how nutritious the food may be. My perception became distorted. Emotional equilibrium disappeared. Worst of all, I lost spiritual contact with a Higher Power.

Maintaining that contact is essential for me. If God is not my first priority, food will be. I have a daily reprieve from compulsive overeating which is dependent on my spiritual condition. When I get out of touch with my Higher Power, I am headed for a binge. Pride and ego take over. I think I can do it on my own. I forget that my goal is to know God's will for me and do it. I get caught up in the illusion and frenzy of self-will which sooner or later leads to excess food.

When I am out of touch with God, I am spiritually hungry. There is a gaping emptiness at the center of my being. I try to fill the emptiness with food, but there is never enough. Finally, the pain of bingeing leads me back to God, and I realize my hunger was not for food but for a spiritual connection.

I pray for the humility to remember I am always incomplete without God. I want to recognize my spiritual hunger for what it is and learn ways of satisfying it directly, instead of getting sidetracked into unsatisfactory substitutes.

When we are spiritually full, our resentments dissolve and we don't need revenge. Getting in touch with God's love enables us to love ourselves and other people. When we are in contact with a Higher Power, we don't feel deprived and we don't need to get even with anyone. We find the source of strength and nurturing that we crave. Since we don't expect other people to "fill us up," we don't get angry with them when they don't meet our every need.

The key to getting rid of resentment is our ability to forgive the people who have hurt or angered us. What makes more sense, to forgive or to let resentment fester and become an excuse for overeating?

I may think I feel a hunger for revenge, but I know trying to satisfy it will harm me more than anyone else. I need to go deeper into myself, beyond the hunger for revenge. First I come to a layer of anger. If I can get through that without overeating and go still deeper, I come to a layer of hurt. Forgiveness is the way through that layer, and it helps to remind myself of all the times I have consciously or unconsciously hurt someone else. I believe my Higher Power forgives me for my mistakes, and I believe it even more firmly when I am able to pass the forgiveness along.

Not long ago my feelings were hurt by someone I care about very much. I felt unloved and neglected, because he made plans to spend a holiday with other friends and not with me.

My first reaction was, "I don't care. I'm not mad. Let him go. I'll find something better to do. I'll find another man. He can be replaced." Making plans to search for the replacement, I thought to myself, "You lose, Buddy. You'll be sorry. I'll make you sorry." Then I went looking for something to eat.

No. I realized that route leads to slow suicide. I began to feel my feelings and listen to what the hunger was telling me. It was telling me I was angry — more than angry — I was enraged! How could he do this to me? Of all the unfeeling, inconsiderate . . . he was not worth my time . . . I would never speak to him again. I hoped disaster would strike like a thunderbolt on his excursion without me.

It was good to feel the anger, but what was I going to do with it? I fumed, and then I fumed some more. And then I listened again.

What else was there inside, prompting me to head for the refrigerator?

I could feel inner tears, burning like a physical pain. I began to let the tears out. It was good to feel the hurt, but what was I going to do with that? I kept going back to the refrigerator, but I didn't eat.

I read, I prayed, I sat, I listened. I felt very uncomfortable. I realized if I continued to pretend to my friend that everything was fine and he should go off with other people and leave me alone for the holiday weekend, I was asking for a sleepless night or a binge or both. What's more, I was cheating myself and the relationship.

Why is it so difficult to say what I feel and ask for what I want? Why would I choose revenge instead of trying to work out a problem? Finally, I picked up the phone and called him. I expressed some anger and some hurt. I spoke and I listened and, over a period of about thirty-six hours, some of which were spent together with my friend, I lost the desire for revenge and figured out some ways of getting my needs met without having to binge or destroy the relationship.

Below my hunger for revenge, below my anger and hurt, there is a deeper hunger: the hunger for relatedness. I crave to feel that I belong, that I am part of humanity and linked in union with all of life. When I get down to this hunger, and I get there by way of abstinence, I arrive at a sense of needing to give out rather than take in. My shoulders relax, I breathe deeply, and I feel my spirit expand rather than contract. I can risk giving love, even if it may be rejected. Eventually the love I give will come back to me. True wealth is having love to give and being able to give it without demanding an immediate equal return.

When I let myself be embraced by the God of my understanding and can reach out to embrace other people, I no longer feel deprived. I have what I need today — more than enough. I always did. And tomorrow? Now I am back to fear. "What is the fear of need but need itself? Is not dread of thirst when your well is full, the thirst that is unquenchable?"[1] I have enough to satisfy my hunger now, but if I don't take things one day at a time, then my hunger is insatiable. I may not always have what I think I want, but I believe that my Higher Power gives me what I need.

Once I get over being mad at God for not having given me horses and a swimming pool and naturally curly hair back when I was ten, I can more fully appreciate the gifts I am given today and every day. Today I don't want a swimming pool or a horse, though I'd still like natural curls. I have love and I have work. I have family and friends, and I have an inner voice that directs me when I listen.

Often that voice tells me I'm hungry, but I'm learning that I'm not really hungry for revenge, or for excess food as a substitute. Revenge is no longer sweet, if it ever was, and it no longer satisfies, if it ever did. Life satisfies, and abstinence is sweet.

If we expect the impossible of ourselves, we are bound to be disappointed.

FOUR

The Skywriter

All of us hunger to achieve. We want to feel a sense of accomplishment. Achievement is important to our self-esteem and comes to us in many areas: work, hobbies, academic studies, sports, community activities. Some of us spread our achievements over a variety of areas, while others tend to zero in on one or two prime targets of accomplishment. Some of us feel frustrated in our efforts to achieve and are haunted by a sense of having failed to accomplish anything of value. Some of us are driven to compulsive work or compulsive play to prove something that is actually out of reach, or to arrive at a goal that forever eludes us.

We all need praise and positive strokes from people whose opinion is important to us. We need frequent affirmations of our worth. We need to feel we are spending our time and energy in productive ways and that our efforts are appreciated. One of our early achievements was learning to feed ourselves. Most likely we were praised for successful efforts, even if they were somewhat uncoordinated at the start.

Were you a member of the clean plate club? Were you praised when you finished all your beans and all your potatoes and all your meatloaf? Were you then allowed to have dessert? Were you cheered on as you got to the bottom of a large glass of milk and assured you would grow to be big and strong if you drank it all? Being able to sit at the dining room table and eat with the grown-ups was "big time" for most of us, though we may have forgotten about it by now.

As we grew, we branched out into new areas of achievement and mastery: talking, riding a tricycle and later a bike, tying shoelaces, learning to count, building a sand castle, playing softball, painting a picture. We went to school and took tests and passed from one grade to the next.

My sixth grade class was in charge of putting together a magazine for the entire elementary school (approximately two hundred students). There were two issues of the magazine each year, one near Christmas and one in late spring. Stories, short articles, and poems were submitted from all the classes, and the sixth grade students picked from among the submissions, did the necessary editing, and assembled the magazine. It was called *The Skywriter*.

I was one of two assistant editors for *The Skywriter*. Together with the editor-in-chief, I sifted through the submissions from each grade and decided what would be in and what would be out. Power! We did it in the fall, and we did it again in the spring.

In terms of psychic income, I believe I reached the peak of my career in the sixth grade. Not only was I the assistant editor of *The Skywriter*, but I was also elected president of the class and had a major part in the sixth grade play, as the princess in *Rumplestiltskin*. Never have I felt so important. I became overbearing and probably alienated my friends, because I remember being very lonely in the seventh grade. My season in the sun was brief, but it was great while it lasted.

As I grew older, it became more and more difficult to attain the performance peaks I craved. I was hungry for power and achievement, but they were increasingly out of reach. Was that part of the reason for polishing off a box of cookies? Somehow the clean plate syndrome became the empty box accomplishment. If I could no longer get elected president of my class, I could eat a large amount of ice cream. Somewhere in the back of my head, somebody was telling me this was the way to be big and strong.

Conflict was inherent, since big and strong was not what made high school girls popular with high school boys. I knew this when I reached for the ice cream carton, but learning how to relate to the opposite sex was difficult, and eating ice cream was easy.

Getting A's was pretty easy, too, in a small high school, and that gave me the feeling of being somewhat on top of things even though I had very few dates. In college, the situation reversed itself — it was easier to get dates and harder to get A's. Unfortunately, overeating was always easy. When I couldn't be an academic star or a musical genius, something inside me could feel I had achieved some obscure goal by eating. That's not very rational, considering that one of my ambitions was to wear a size eight.

I had a fierce need to make a mark, preferably in giant letters across the sky. I wanted to be perfect, to be powerful, to be on top, to win. I wasn't sure what the rules were, or even the name of the game, but my ambition to win knew no bounds. I fed it with food. When success was not forthcoming, I fed it some more. The more I ate, the less I achieved (except the production of fat).

Achievement is hard. Eating is easy. Eating recalls past achievement in early years and becomes a substitute for current accomplishment in the here and now.

Listen to the hunger. What do you want to achieve? Do you want to go back to school and get a degree? Would you like to start your own business? Have you always wanted to learn how to ski? Do you feel your present job is a dead end, and are you staying in it because that's easier than looking for a new one?

When you think about taking action to fulfill one of your ambitions, do you get scared or discouraged and decide to have something to eat? All too often, an overeater will choose the immediate, short-term gratification of food instead of working toward a long-term goal.

33

Acknowledging our desires and dreams is the first step toward realizing them. Sit down and take time to think about three specific goals you want to accomplish by this time next year. Write them down on paper. For example,

1) a more interesting job
2) a better relationship with a family member
3) a firmer body
4) improved self-esteem

Now, outline the concrete steps you will take this week to make progress toward your goals. For number one, you might decide to find out about getting some career counseling or help with preparing a resume. Number two might be making plans to go bowling with your son tomorrow night. Number three might be starting an exercise program today. Most of us who have eating disorders are low on self-esteem, so how about some professional help if a support group isn't enough?

It is unlikely that any of our goals will be furthered by eating more than what is necessary for good health. But how many of us crave food when we start thinking about a project we want to do but are apprehensive about tackling? Reading the classified ads for employment makes me feel hungry. When I sit down and analyze the feeling, it turns out to be anxiety rather than hunger. I will not find a job in the refrigerator. Nor will I be able to escape for long the necessity of working to pay my bills by burying my face in a box of crackers.

If my desired accomplishments are too grandiose and unrealistic, I will be easily discouraged. I need to set realistic goals, often in small steps so that reaching one will encourage me to move on to the next. Where did I get the idea I am supposed to be perfect? That defeats me before I start. Not many of us are superstars, and not many of us are miserable failures. Most of us fall somewhere in between, and we need to affirm our modest achievements. Chances are I will never be the chairman of the board or Miss America, but I probably can be a competent administrative assistant who is physically fit and justifiably proud of both accomplishments. Chances are I will continue to make mistakes as a mother, but I can work on better communication with my children and be glad about the times when I do things right.

What works against me in the achievement of realistic goals is compulsive overeating. That little extra bit of food which is supposed to make things better always makes them worse. Arrogantly, I think "This time I can get away with it," but I never can. You know what I mean if you have passed the point of no return in using food to fill emotional needs and solve problems food cannot solve. At one time we may have had control over how much extra we ate, but that control is no longer there. One definition of an alcoholic is a person who cannot safely drink. A compulsive overeater is someone who cannot safely snack. The extra bites become binges, and goals go down the drain.

At one time I thought eating more food would give me extra strength to tackle a hard job. In the past, I used the quick energy from high-carbohydrate foods to get me through a difficult or unpleasant task, especially when I was tired. Excess food as a stimulant, however, does not work very well. The quick burst of energy is followed by fatigue. My body needs to be properly nourished if I am to achieve my goals, but overeating produces diminishing returns. The more I eat, the less I am able to do. If I listen to the hunger signals when I think I need extra food for extra strength, I often discover my real hunger is for rest.

Perfectionism is my enemy when it drives me beyond my strength to the point where fatigue threatens my abstinence. Doing a good job is within my reach. Being perfect is not. Setting my goals too high invites me to give up.

Perfectionism can also be the enemy of abstinence. Abstaining from compulsive overeating is probably more difficult than abstaining from alcohol or other drugs, because we cannot abstain from food completely. We have to come to terms with moderation three times a day. We may have slips. The desire to do it perfectly can be an excuse for giving up and allowing a small slip to escalate into a major binge.

The God of my understanding does not expect me to be perfect. I think my Higher Power expects me to do the best I can. It's my will that gets me into the trap of perfectionism, my will wanting to run the show and my overblown ego wanting to take control.

Praying only for the knowledge of God's will for me and the power to carry that out gets me away from the trap and back to the real world. Without humility, I'm not likely to be abstinent for very long. I need to remember I'm not perfect and I'm not God. With humility, I can ask for and receive the help I need to set goals and take steps to reach them. Extra food doesn't do it; God does.

We all like applause and pats on the back. As we get older, hopefully we become increasingly able to *give* pats on the back as well as receive them. Hopefully, we also develop a growing ability to affirm ourselves when we act according to the directions of an inner voice, whether or not praise is forthcoming from outside.

When our hunger to achieve is nourished and guided by a Higher Power, the result is emotional and spiritual growth. There is challenge, adventure, and the satisfaction of feeling part of something larger than ourselves. Paradoxically, the most power and the greatest achievements come through surrender. I didn't know that in the sixth grade. I still forget it fairly often. Maybe I should write it in giant letters across my ceiling.

When we are plugged into our Higher Power, we are plugged into love. It flows through us like a current, energizing our sluggish hearts and minds.

FIVE

Dancing Lessons

I desperately wanted to go to dancing school when I was eleven, because most of my friends were going. In particular, the boy I had a crush on was going, and so was another girl who also had a crush on him. She would have an unfair advantage, and I would lose out! How much of an advantage going to dancing school actually was, I'm not sure, but the other girl did capture the attentions of the boy, and I consoled myself by baking cakes and eating them. Another boy, who also went to dancing school, had a crush on me, but he was not the one I wanted. By the time I got interested in him several years later, he had lost interest in me.

When I was twelve, I was allowed to go to dancing school, and I had a miserable time. I was a head taller than most of the boys and had a bigger waistline than most of the girls. I continued to bake and eat cakes.

While I ate, I fantasized about the glamorous, exotic male who would sweep me into his arms and make me live happily ever after. All I knew for sure about him was that he would be tall, dark, and handsome and, of course, devoted to me.

I didn't meet anyone like that in dancing school. The closest approximation (whom I would happily have accepted) never asked me to dance, although we were frequent partners when the class paired off according to height. Through a neighbor, I did meet an exotic male who was dark but not very tall. This man was renting a room in my neighbor's house. He came from an Eastern European country and was more than twice my age. He, the neighbors, my parents, and I played canasta, and I was wild about him, but we never danced. I would sometimes catch a glimpse of him through the kitchen window of our house. While I watched for him, I ate cookies.

I spent a lot of time wishing and fantasizing and eating, but I was never the belle of the ball. I spent a lot of time being a wallflower, feeling embarrassed and conspicuous and envying my more popular girlfriends. When the older brother of a boy in my dancing class asked me for a date, I was flattered and quite scared. I was almost fifteen. He was almost seventeen. We went to the movies. I didn't hear from him again for six months. Then we went to a party, and he kissed me, and it was not at all the way I had imagined my first kiss would be. It was anything but chaste, and I was both shocked and fascinated. We dated for about six years, mainly during vacations, since he went away to high school and I later went away to college.

We went to many dances. The slow music we managed just fine, but we never could handle a jitterbug. That was probably because I had no confidence in my ability to jitterbug and was too proud to ask for help. Most of the dancing school group had gone on to advanced classes, where they learned how to jitterbug, but I had piano lessons instead.

The man I married was the first partner I could follow on the dance floor when the music was fast. The first time we tried, the fact that I had had a drink or two undoubtedly loosened me up and dissolved some of my self-consciousness. We danced together quite well for about ten years before we began to get out of step. By then I could jitterbug with almost anyone.

All my life, I think I have been learning to dance. From the preschool ballet class, where my performance was anything but outstanding, to a recent adult education class in disco dancing, moving to music has been a metaphor for living. I like to think I am freer now to express who I am and what I feel through the music and rhythms of dance.

We dance our way into and out of love affairs and relationships, delighted and transported when the rhythm is shared, frustrated and unhappy when the steps don't mesh. Dancing with a partner is harder than dancing alone, but when the rhythm is right, I would say it's much more fun to have a partner.

Romance. Relationship. Love. Sex. Dancing is a prelude to intimacy. Dancing is nonverbal communication. Initially, two bodies communicate with each other. When the outcome is positive, the dancing continues and the communication deepens. When each partner stays responsive and open to the other, the dance goes on indefinitely, sometimes faster, sometimes slower, sometimes closer, sometimes with more space between the two, but always with relatedness.

If we stop being responsive to each other, the rhythm is broken and communication gets cut off or becomes garbled. If we change partners, we usually find we're still learning to dance and still working on many of the same patterns and steps that tripped us up in the past. Perfect partners are hard to find. If that's what we're looking for, we may find ourselves dancing alone most of the time.

When I was growing up, sex was a hunger I thought I shouldn't have. Romance, relationship, and love were just fine, but sex was definitely problematic. "Nice girls don't." That was the message, spoken and unspoken. So I ate cookies. I started having secret sugar-eating sessions when I was eleven. That was when I wanted to go to dancing school. That same year I began to wear bras and started menstruating. Through puberty, adolescence, and young adulthood, I often confused hunger for sex with hunger for food.

At one time, I thought sexual satisfaction was the cure for compulsive overeating. That would have been a nice, simple solution, but it didn't work for me. Sexual satisfaction is great, and without it I am frustrated, but it's not enough. It

41

doesn't fill all of my hunger. There is much more. Mechanical sex without some degree of love and tenderness is probably impossible for most of us. The more love and caring and commitment that goes along with the expression of sex, the more completely we are filled.

A committed, caring, loving sexual relationship goes a long way toward satisfying my hunger, but even that is not enough. My dancing partner can't be expected to meet all my needs all the time. The only way I can hope to stay in step with another person is by letting a Higher Power be the ultimate leader, the "Lord of the Dance."

When God is leading, I can risk being open and vulnerable. If my partner lets me down, I will be hurt, but I will not be devastated. I can go back to my inner core and find peace and strength and direction. When God is leading, I will not be so overly dependent on my partner that I lean too hard and either we both fall or my partner gets tired of trying to prop me up and leaves.

I think the ideal situation is where both partners acknowledge a Higher Power as Lord of the Dance and in charge of their relationship. They then have an ever-present third party to keep them in step with the music and rhythm of their lives together.

There are many ways in which we divert our life-enhancing hunger for love into dead-end detours. We can have compulsive sex with a variety of partners, or even with the same partner, and use that as a way of avoiding the challenge of an emotionally and spiritually intimate relationship. We can get ourselves involved in a love affair with alcohol or other drugs, anesthetizing sensations and feelings and dissipating the energy that could go into building a nurturing relationship. Compulsive work can be a substitute for intimacy. And, of course, so can compulsive overeating.

If we're afraid of physical and/or emotional intimacy, we can try to protect ourselves with a wall of fat. The protection is self-defeating, since our real needs are not being met. The more we eat, the lonelier we get. The lonelier we get, the more we eat. We can be part of a family and know many people and still be lonely. It's the quality of our relationships that determines whether or not they fill our needs for love and intimacy. If we are not able to honestly identify and share our feelings, we are going to be lonely, no matter how many people are around.

How do we break out of the prison of emotional isolation? Overeaters can learn to reach for people instead of food. We learn we may have to make the first move, even if we risk rejection. If you are alone at three o'clock on a Sunday afternoon, and thinking about eating food, which your body doesn't need, in order to try to make yourself feel better emotionally, stop! Is there someone close by you can talk to? If not, phone someone. Eating food you don't need will make you feel worse. Making contact with a friend will make you feel better. If the first person you talk to doesn't help, try someone else. Try talking to someone with the idea of making *that* person feel better!

We need friends as well as dancing partners. One special man can't do everything for a woman, just as one special woman can't do everything for a man. A girl who grows up believing in the Prince Charming myth is particularly vulnerable to unrealistic expectations and subsequent disappointments. If we're completely dependent on one person for emotional sustenance, we're going to be in sad shape when that person is not available or does not come through with what we expect and want.

Having several good friends whom we can talk to on a deep, meaningful level enriches us and means we don't have to make impossible demands on a love relationship. It makes sense to invest the time and energy required to build nourishing friendships. A closed, one-to-one, exclusive relationship can dry up for lack of outside contacts. When we have other good friends, we have more to give to that special person.

What happens when you don't have a partner? More and more of us are single these days. We may or may not be involved in a relationship. Sometimes we'd love to dance but no one asks us. We may do the asking ourselves and get turned down. Let's remind ourselves that one is a whole number. I may not choose to be alone but find myself alone regardless. Rather than desperately latching on to the first available partner I can find, I would prefer to assume that God's plan for my life at this precise moment is for me to be single and alone, for the time being.

Besides, I never need to be completely alone. There are many different kinds of relationships besides romantic ones, many different groups of dancers I can join. The question for me to answer has to do with where my Higher Power is leading me. The way I handle my hunger for relatedness will let me know if I am getting off the track. If I am slipping back into the habit of consuming food instead of giving love, then I am out of touch with God and going in the wrong direction.

What happens when you have a partner but your partner doesn't want to dance with you? Perhaps you feel this person doesn't seem to want to communicate on the level you would like or is dancing to different music. There's one course of action we can definitely rule out — overeating. My built-in response to conflict and frustration was to try to make the unpleasantness go away with food. I hated confrontation, so I would ignore my feelings until either they exploded or I had buried them under an avalanche of food.

I am learning how to identify what I am feeling — anger, fear, hurt, loneliness, exasperation, despair — and then be responsible for doing something about it. I cannot change my partner. I can let him know how I feel, and I can talk about what I would like him to do, but what he does is up to him and his Higher Power. I cannot change him, but I can change my response to him. If I don't like the way he dances, I can either accept him as he is and decide I want to continue to work on improving the relationship (perhaps with some outside help), or I can decide I don't want to be his partner.

Since overeaters tend to feel guilty about overeating, we may allow ourselves to become doormats and take more than our share of responsibility for an ailing relationship. This is as disastrous as placing all of the blame on the other person. As the saying goes, "It takes two to tango." What we are trying to do is learn how to move together in a rhythm that pleases us both. If we get stuck trying to figure out who's most responsible for the missteps, we'll never get on with the dance.

Interestingly enough, it seems to me that when I have my own act together I get along much better with my partner. When I'm out of sync internally and out of touch with my center, the inner discord spills out into my relationship with the other person. If I'm out of rhythm with the Lord of the Dance, I'm out of step with my partner, too.

When the rhythm is broken, the best thing for me to do is turn the situation over and get back to the idea of God's will instead of my will. God knows better than I the strengths and weaknesses of my partner, and God loves this person even more than I do. I need to be sure I am doing everything possible to make the relationship work before I give up based on an inventory of my partner's faults and defects.

For a long time I have known how to put food in my mouth, but I'm still learning how to dance. I need to keep practicing the Steps and not be misled into thinking that more food will be a satisfactory substitute for the physical, emotional, and spiritual love I crave. If music is the sound of love, then dancing is a metaphor for its rhythm and pattern. I need to know when to keep moving and when to sit down and rest, when to come close to my partner and when to back off and allow him space.

As we grow, we learn how to move freely and at the same time avoid stepping on each other's toes (most of the time).

As we become more graceful, we can express our own feelings without injuring the other person. We can learn how to give each other room to breathe and still maintain an intimate relationship. When a Higher Power leads, we both can follow with complementary movements.

Don't settle for eating cookies. Wouldn't you rather dance?

As we improve our contact with our Higher Power, we find ourselves less and less despondent. We have new hope, faith, and love— all powerful antidotes to depression.

SIX

The Black Hole

I spent one summer doing very little other than playing solitaire and eating. There were people around me much of the time — my husband, two children, neighbors, friends, and acquaintances — so I wasn't eating and playing solitaire for lack of available company. I was the one who withdrew. I'm not sure why, but nothing seemed worthwhile. I trudged through my daily routine, doing the necessary household duties with great effort and feeling incapable of generating enthusiasm for anything.

Depression. I was down in the bottom of a black hole, struggling to get out but not finding the exit. Food gave me a temporary lift until the overload of calories sedated me and I went to sleep. I shuffled cards, binged, and slept all summer long. It was as though the productive part of me had gone on strike.

When September came, I joined Overeaters Anonymous. For several years, I had resisted O.A., since I could not imagine giving up my sugary snacks. If there had been anything else left to try I would have continued to resist, but I had run out of alternatives. There was no place else to go, and I didn't want to spend the rest of my life in a black hole with a deck of cards.

That was ten years ago. I wish I could say I was lifted out of the hole once and for all and I never experienced any more darkness. What I can say is that my periods of depression since then have been much more brief, that the darkness has not been so black, and that I have not played solitaire. I can also say that I now can see unmistakable signs of significant growth which has occurred during the dark times.

The black hole has an exit, but to get out I have to go through the darkness and let myself be surrounded by it and immersed in it. Trying to get around the darkness just makes it bigger, and the trip takes more time, because after going all the way around I still have to go through the blackness.

Instead of a hole, I now like to think of the dark place as a womb. When I surrender to the emptiness and the sadness it contains, I am nourished and made ready for the next stage in my spiritual and emotional journey.

I had been separated from my former husband for about a year, and it was winter when I found myself back in one of those dark places. There was such a gaping emptiness, a void at the center of my being. I was hollow. Can it be that inner space is as vast as outer space? Is there a link? Exploring inner space is an adventure, and courage is required when one decides to make the expedition.

C.G. Jung writes,

> This path to the primordial religious experience is the right one, but how many can recognize it? It is like a still small voice, and it sounds from afar. It is ambiguous, questionable, dark, presaging danger and hazardous adventure; a razor-edged path, to be trodden for God's sake only, without assurance and without sanction.[1]

And André Gide observes, "One doesn't discover new lands without consenting to lose sight of the shore for a very long time."[2]

As I became willing to feel the emptiness, not fight it or frantically try to fill it up but just experience it, I gradually began to lose my fear of the void inside myself. Instead of being a thing of terror, it became soft and quiet and a source of peace. I could let myself sink into the emptiness and be nurtured by its vastness. The darkness became restful, like the experience of leaving the hot outdoors and entering a cool room with the shades drawn. I resigned myself to being empty and sad and alone. Out of the acceptance of nothingness came a kind of serenity and a strong sense of being supported by a Higher Power. The emptiness wasn't really empty. Slowly it began to be filled with new growth, and slowly the darkness lifted.

We don't see what is happening to the seed planted in the dark earth until it sprouts and pushes up through the surface. The darkness nourishes the seed. The womb nourishes the fetus. Similarly, creativity arises out of inner emptiness and space. While our creative spirit is lying dormant, we may think nothing is going on. We become bored and frustrated and depressed. We think we should never feel empty. We're afraid of the void.

One of the ways to try to fix emotional and spiritual emptiness is to translate it into physical hunger and attempt to fill the inner void with food. There is never enough food to do the job, because food won't fill emotional and spiritual emptiness. It seems to be a fact that we all experience dry spells, times when enthusiasm and motivation apparently disappear. Mystics talk about the "dark night of the soul." Just as day alternates with night in our physical world, so too our moods fluctuate, and we go through periods of light and dark in our spiritual journey. Trying to avoid the lows with chemicals or excess food does not work.

What usually occurs is that the temporary high is followed by an even lower low than the one we were trying to cure with a substance. When we overeat in an attempt to ward off depression, the long-term result is more depression.

When you're feeling really low, and food appears to be the only solution, how do you discover what the hunger is really about? Have there been times when your emotional world seemed so black that you just didn't care about anything? You knew bingeing would make you feel even worse, but so

51

what? Do you get to a point where you'd say, "To hell with everything, I'm going to eat"? What was the hunger telling you?

The summer when I ate and played solitaire, I think my hunger was telling me I was spiritually starved. I didn't know that then. I only knew I was committing slow suicide and I had to do something. Looking back, I can see my emotions and my spirit were malnourished. I had no real friends. I was not communicating with my family except on a very superficial level, and I did not have the kind of faith in a Higher Power that could make a difference in my day-to-day life. I did what I had to do as my part of maintaining the household, but that was all. I tried to hide most of my negative feelings with a deck of cards and high-calorie carbohydrates. Emotionally I was on strike, and spiritually I was just about dead.

For me, the breakthrough occurred when spiritual hunger overcame inertia and prompted me to look for help beyond the walls of my kitchen. In retrospect, I can see that all through my life a Power greater than myself has led me out of dark places when I have been ready to turn toward the light. The light is always there, but we don't always see it. That summer I looked for help and found the Twelve Step programs.

Going to meetings was like finding an oasis in my desert of isolation. I went to O.A. meetings and A.A. meetings. I was ready to accept the fact that nothing short of a spiritual awakening was going to lift me out of depression. That didn't come about all of a sudden, but gradually the days began to have meaning and there was motivation to do something besides play solitaire.

I took telephone numbers and I called people. I stopped drinking. I wrote down a food plan and followed it. I no longer went to bed with the idea that I would rather not wake up the next morning. When I did wake up, it was with a feeling of lightness and enthusiasm — yes, I was abstinent!

I talked to my new friends about how I really felt, the hidden things that bothered me. I began to get honest with myself and take inventory. I shared the inventory and felt released from a heavy burden. I took the risk of looking for a job and found one.

All of that did not happen overnight. My recovery has taken years and is still ongoing. The dark times continue to come, and I sometimes seem to go backwards into the place where food looks like the answer. The difference now is that I have a better idea of where to look for help. I can go to a meeting; I can meditate; I can sit still and feel the hunger until I can put a name on it.

Isolating ourselves makes us emotionally hungry. We need meaningful contact with other people. We may see and talk to family and friends every day but not be communicating in a way that satisfies our hunger. We need at least one person in our lives with whom we can be completely open and honest.

Depression is frozen anger, anger at other people and anger at ourselves. To get out of the depression, we first have to recognize and own the anger. Taking a Fourth Step inventory helped me see where my anger was coming from and how it had me immobilized. I was on strike because I was mad. Being able to talk about my anger in the safe environment of a support group was the next step in moving out of the black hole.

The time comes for all of us, however, when we're talked out. At that point, the most positive course of action is to turn the black hole and all of its contents over to a Higher Power. We can become willing to give up depression in the same way we give up our other character defects. By the time we get through an inventory, we're probably aware that if we were less self-centered we'd be less depressed. As long as we're focusing on what we want, we're going to feel empty and see clouds. Light breaks through when we begin to change our perspective and start thinking about what God wants.

Each time we go down into our inner darkness, we can learn a little more about ourselves and our Higher Power. We'd rather not have the kind of learning experience that involves feeling lost and depressed. However, accepting the negative feelings when they come works better than trying to ward them off by overeating. Excess food only makes the depression last longer. (It should be noted that a continuing, severe depression requires professional treatment. If in doubt, consult a physician or therapist. My own recovery has included professional therapy, which has been enormously helpful.)

There was a big difference between the black hole I was in during the summer when I played solitaire and in the winter when I was sad and empty. In the first case, I tried to ignore my feelings and cover them up with food and compulsive activity. In the second case, after several years of working the Twelve Steps, I was able to accept the dark place I was in, feel my feelings, and wait for new light and new growth.

There have been other dark times for me. Sometimes the black hole is a mood that lasts for a few hours, and sometimes it continues much longer. Hunger is part of it. I know now that my hunger has a spiritual component which requires more than calories. When I sit and listen to the hunger that comes out of my inner darkness, I hear a cry for help. I need to be reconnected to the light, to the Power greater than myself.

I can't get around dark times, but I can pass through them and know they are stages on my spiritual journey and there is growth on the other side. When I become willing to ask for help, I am no longer alone and empty. I don't need to play solitaire.

Prayer is not so much telling and asking as it is listening.

SEVEN

Peace Like a River

We hunger for security, for accomplishment, for love, for adventure, for spiritual growth. Our hunger reflects and expresses our needs, and our needs pyramid one on top of the other. We satisfy one hunger, and we move on to the next, and we go back to the beginning and do it again.

Do you think underneath all the striving, the wanting, the doing, and the moving, we each have a deep, basic hunger for peace? Is that what some of the eating is about? How effective a tranquilizer is food? Isn't there a better way to settle our restlessness and our anxiety?

Food is a temporary tranquilizer. We can eat ourselves into a kind of oblivion where we no longer feel or care. We can eat so much that we literally pass out. We can put ourselves to sleep with a binge. However, we may wake up in the middle of the night with an upset stomach, a racing mind, and the sweats.

How do we find the peace we crave? Before I got into the Twelve Step programs, I was not unfamiliar with prayer and meditation. Sunday school and church were a regular part of my life until I went to college, where my participation in religious organizations became less regular. I did believe in a Higher Power, and I often asked for help, but the God of my understanding at that time was remote.

I needed help. Instead of going to sleep at night, I would find myself in the middle of a panic attack with my mind in confusion, my heart pounding, my fingers tingling, and a terrifying sense of being unable to breathe. I was bingeing regularly, sometimes stealing food from the dorm kitchen and from other people's rooms. I was drinking coffee all day long and late into the night, and I was smoking like a chimney.

I was a freshman when my doctor prescribed tranquilizers, and I took them regularly for twenty-one years until I joined O.A. and started working the program. Within less than three years, I was also able to do without caffeine, alcohol, sugar, and laxatives.

Our timing varies in the program. Abstinence comes to some almost immediately, while others struggle on and off for years. Most discover that maintaining spiritual contact is the key to being abstinent. Only by daily surrender to a Higher Power am I able to experience the deep peace and faith that make overeating unnecessary.

Peace comes to me when I am willing to accept life unconditionally. As long as I think I know what's best and as long as I insist on trying to make people and events conform to my will, I am going to be swimming upstream, thrashing about with much effort but making little progress. Through prayer and meditation, I begin to get a sense of something beyond my strength, my will, and my knowledge which is supporting and guiding me. When I can say, "Okay, God, You take over," and when I can accept what happens, then I know peace.

I believe we all experience spiritual discontent until we are able to feel connected to a Power greater than ourselves, the God of our understanding. We may not always be able to identify our discontent as spiritual hunger. That's when we keep on chasing the pipe dreams of this world, convinced that satisfaction lies in the next drink, the next bite, the next love, the next thousand dollars.

We'd like to feel that satisfaction is within our control. This makes it difficult to accept the paradox that surrender — giving up the illusion of control — is the path to lasting satisfaction. What we want, what we think will satisfy us, changes with our moods and will probably be different tomorrow or next week. Deciding to let God manage our lives relieves us of the burden and pain of self-will, which is continually going to be frustrated since self-will is uncertain and since there are so many circumstances beyond our control.

I look back and see that the separate pieces of my life have fit together to form a meaningful pattern. One event has led to another. One door has closed so another could open. It makes sense. While the events were happening I was often anxious and perplexed. Worrying about the future robbed me of peace in the present. In reality, I have no control over whether or not the sun will rise tomorrow, nor can I control what the days, weeks, and years ahead will bring to me. What I can do is learn to trust God's pattern as it unfolds one day at a time.

Surrendering my will and seeking conscious contact with a Higher Power brings me the peace which goes beyond understanding. It is not something I can grasp and define with my mind but a feeling that permeates my entire being.

This peace I experience when I am in contact with my center is not static. It flows, moving me through my daily activities with both energy and serenity. It is a sense that all is right with my world, because I am resting in the heart of God. There is nothing to fear, because I am being supported and directed. When I feel this kind of peace and oneness with my environment, I don't crave extra food. There is no sense of needing more, because I have what is necessary and I feel complete.

When I experience great elation, rather than feeling peaceful, I fear and know the high won't last. This is because the high itself carries a charge of overstimulation that is not tranquil. Deep depression is not peaceful either, since I am fighting pain and sadness. Peace is somewhere between, or outside of, the highs and the lows. It is "a condition of complete simplicity, costing not less than everything."[1] It is acceptance of the things I cannot change. It is giving up the things I wanted to have but which I really don't need and which are only in my way. What is peace worth to you?

The peace we crave cannot be commanded, but it can be nurtured. We can set aside quiet times during the day and practice being in the presence of a Higher Power. Consciously letting go of whatever is bothering us allows us to gain a new perspective.

The God of my understanding is outside time and space but accessible to me only in the immediacy of the present moment. If that sounds like a contradiction, please remember that what I am trying to describe is more than can be defined with logic and intellect. We need to be willing to move beyond the limited rationality of our minds and experience the unlimited capabilities of our spirits.

At first, when we begin a regular program of prayer and meditation, we will probably only get snatches of serenity, bits and pieces of peaceful feelings. We might start with ten minutes in the morning and ten minutes at night. It often helps to use a meditation book to get started, but we should allow time to just sit quietly and be in the presence of God. This quiet time when we are apparently doing nothing can expand to become everything, a world of peace.

These quiet periods serve as touchstones for the other hours of the day. They anchor us. When circumstances come up in which we feel distressed and upset, we can go back in our minds and hearts to the quiet times and extract a measure of peace to counteract our distress. We know that below the surface of what appears to be a disastrous situation, there is a deeper calm.

Do you think that you can make a muddy pool clean?
Be still and the mud will settle.[2]

Be still and know that I am God.[3]

Teach us to care and not to care.
Teach us to sit still.[4]

Another paradox: The peace we thought we could get from food comes when we abstain from overeating. Think about that. You're upset. You want to be soothed. You eat something and it makes you feel a little better. You eat something more, and more, and more, until feeling better begins to feel worse, but you can't stop eating. That makes you scared. You don't like yourself, and you are not at peace.

Being abstinent does not mean we will be permanently tranquil. We will experience the tension and stress of everyday life, and we will feel it more acutely without the buffer of excess food. The peace of abstinence is what we feel below the stress. It lifts our spirits with the knowledge that we can cope with whatever the day brings as long as we don't take the first compulsive bite.

For me, there is no real peace without abstinence and no abstinence without a Higher Power.

Abstinence means being selective about how we satisfy our legitimate hunger and need for food. We select what will be most nourishing to our bodies, and we avoid foods which do not supply the nutrients we need. To be abstinent is to make choices which promote physical health and well-being.

My choice has been to avoid refined sugar, alcohol, and caffeine, all of which make me feel "jangled" and less than serene. These substances give me a temporary lift and some artificial excitement, but eventually deplete my energy and make me feel I am spinning my wheels.

What we put into our bodies, and what we do with them, affects emotional equilibrium as well as physical health. In order to satisfy our hunger for peace and serenity, we need to be selective in all of our activities. If we think we should have it all, we will never be at peace. The longer I'm in a Twelve Step program, the easier it is to focus on the priorities in my life and let go of the things I don't really need to do or have. What I'm aiming for might be called abstinence from compulsive overactivity.

I used to be continually frustrated because there were never enough hours in the day to do all the things I wanted to do and thought I was supposed to do. What I actually did wasn't very effective, since I was usually preoccupied with the next item looming ahead on my overcrowded agenda. Worst of all, I was never sure just what it was I wanted to do. What was I missing? What had I left out?

Learning to listen to an inner voice, that still, small voice, quells indecision and frantic activity. When I shift my focus from wondering whether or not life is pleasing me to whether or not I am pleasing life and my Higher Power, I stop thinking I should be able to have it all and do it all. Listening for guidance throughout each day keeps me on track and gives me quiet confidence. The direction comes from inside, enabling me to be selective and not be overwhelmed by conflicting demands and enticements.

However, I frequently get lost and tired and frazzled. I find myself thinking about something to eat. If it's not mealtime, what I need is to get inside a room by myself with the door shut and the telephone and any other noisemakers turned off. When I've lost the sound of my inner voice, I need to be quiet until I can hear it again.

Being at peace doesn't mean sitting around all day like a couch potato doing nothing. Being at peace means being able to move from one activity to the next without rush or undue anxiety. It means being able to act spontaneously in response to what each day brings. When we trust the overall goodness of God's plan, we can go with the flow and not be paralyzed with worry about outcomes.

Peace like a river carries me through difficult times as well as good ones. It makes me feel so much better than ice cream ever did! It makes me flexible — more open to the challenges and gifts of the moment than when I was trying to operate on a rigid schedule aimed at making things go my way, which they rarely did. Inner peace enables me to let others go their way; I make fewer attempts to manipulate and control. When a crisis comes, such as the possibility of losing my job, I am able to face the problem, figure out what action I can take, take it, and leave the results to God.

Another paradox: I find peace through times of quiet, solitary meditation, and I find it in the fellowship of all of you who work the Steps and are recovering. Inner peace, like the program itself, is kept and enhanced by being shared. After a day of conflict and demands, the best thing for me to do may be to go to a meeting or call a friend so my frustration can be expressed and released. Knowing that I have been heard and understood allows me to get back to my center and pass my strength on to someone else.

Our hunger for peace is a life-serving one. The peace on earth for which we pray comes through individuals who find peace within themselves and share it. We know overeating is not the answer to our unrest — abstinence works much better. What is peace worth to you?

We begin to satisfy our hunger for peace when we decide to surrender our will to a Higher Power and accept life unconditionally, without boxing ourselves in with expectations. We nurture inner peace with quiet periods each day for meditating and listening. We move with ease and effectiveness when we get in contact with our Higher Power and let the river of goodness carry us along.

Sometimes we have to spend time hurting before we are able to pass through one phase in our development and move on to the next.

EIGHT

Willing to Feel

WOW!
OUCH!
I'm alive.
Now I feel great and now I hurt.

When you skinned your knee, did someone give you a lollipop to make the hurt go away? Were there times when you were afraid to feel too good in case something bad would come along and spoil everything? Did you get the message that strong feelings were not to be trusted or expressed? Did you decide to keep your feelings to yourself so no one would make fun of you or find out you were vulnerable? Did you learn to eat instead of feel?

I didn't want to feel pain. I didn't want to be angry. I was afraid to experience joy, because it might evaporate and then I would be sad, and I didn't want to be sad. When I was growing up, life seemed to run more smoothly when I was okay, so when I wasn't okay I pretended I was. The easiest way to pretend everything was fine was to have something to eat. If my parents were fighting at the dinner table, I could concentrate on eating my meat, potatoes, and vegetables so I could have dessert. The dessert would make me think I felt better even if the fighting didn't stop.

Later on, when it was Saturday night and I didn't have a date, I could pretend I didn't really care. I had a good book and a half-gallon of ice cream. What more did I need? I knew there was more, but I didn't know how to get it. I used

65

food and fantasy as a substitute for feeling emotions and experiencing real life.

Have you ever heard any of the following comments? "You don't want that." "That doesn't hurt." "You can't be hungry now — it's not time for lunch." "You're too big to be afraid of the dark." "That's not a good book for you to read." "It's not nice to be angry." "Don't play with Dick. He's not the kind of friend you should have." "It's too cold to go out without a sweater." "Of course you want to go to college." "It's time for you to get married and settle down." "No need to be sad. Forget about him and have a good time."

If other people do our feeling for us while we're growing up, we have a difficult time distinguishing what's really going on internally. We don't learn to trust our emotional responses. If you're four years old and afraid of the dark and a parent tells you you're *not* afraid, you come to the conclusion that your feelings are unreliable, since your powerful parent must know more than you do.

Many of us go into adulthood distrustful of our feelings and often unaware of what they are. We think we're supposed to feel a certain way and are uncomfortable if we do not. We try to talk ourselves into responding the way we think we should. It's painful to feel lonely or angry, but if these are our feelings we need to identify them and allow them to surface. We have resources that we didn't have when we were children; we can tolerate some uncomfortable feelings. We can also take steps to do something about them once we're aware of them.

Unfortunately, because of powerful feelings that were too much for us to cope with at the time, we may have learned to short-circuit emotional reactions into false hunger signals. Instead of allowing ourselves to feel loneliness or anger or embarrassment, we immediately translate the unpleasant feelings into hunger. In this way we mask our true emotions and hide them from everyone, including ourselves.

If we overeat instead of recognizing that we're lonely and scared, we are unable to manage the feelings in a constructive way. When we were younger we may not have had much help in dealing with those emotions, and so we did the best we could to feel better, which was to eat. If food was available, it became our coping mechanism.

As adults, what will happen to us if we stop hiding out in excess food and decide to face life? What happens when we choose to take our experiences head on without an anesthetic to dull the unavoidable pain? How do we become willing to feel, and what happens when we do? Listen to your hunger. Let it tell you what's really going on. The next time you have an urge to eat something when you just finished a meal an hour earlier, go behind the hunger and find out what's there.

Are you willing to try? One way to begin is to keep a journal of what you are doing and feeling when you experience a craving for something to eat. Write *before* you eat, even if all you can do is jot down a few words on the back of an envelope. Later on you can transfer the information to your journal and elaborate on it. We're not talking here about normal hunger signals preceding a mealtime. What we're after are the false signals that have more to do with emotional needs than physical hunger for food.

I can give you some examples from my recent experiences. Some days there are many times when I have a feeling of emptiness and an urge to go looking for something to eat. If I give in to the urge, I don't learn anything about the hunger. If I stay with it, I often discover something I didn't know, a flash of insight that tells me what the hunger is really about.

* * * *

10:00 a.m. I am at work. I have shuffled papers around and done the easy, routine tasks that needed immediate attention. Now I have a report to write, and it won't be easy. I've been putting it off for a couple of days, and I've promised myself the first draft will be done by noon today. I sharpen two pencils and I feel hungry. I had breakfast, but I am thinking about lunch. If I were at home I'd be wanting to go to the refrigerator. There is no food in my office, but I am thinking food instead of report.

The task at hand is difficult, and I wonder if I can do it. I am anxious. I don't want to do it. I want to escape into the soothing activity of chewing and swallowing. How many times in the past did I binge when faced with writing a paper for school? Studying for an exam? Balancing my checkbook? Countless times.

I'd like my work to be easy. I feel satisfaction when I've completed a hard job, but I don't like the anxiety of contemplating the task and getting started. Given a large income, big enough clothes, and a society which valued fat women, I'd probably opt for eating chocolates and reading novels. At any rate, that's what I think when I have to do something challenging in order to pay my bills.

It's as though I lapse back to when I was in the first grade and thought I'd never learn to read. Anxiety. "I can't. I won't be good enough. I'll never be able to write the report," is somewhere back in my head. "If I don't write the report, I won't keep my job, and I won't pay the rent, and I'll be a failure." Fear. And food is supposed to help? What helps is reminding myself that I've written reports before and that the way it's done is putting words on paper, one word at a time. It probably won't be the best report ever produced in my organization, but all my Higher Power expects me to do is the best I can today.

3:00 p.m. The report is done. The craving strikes again. The vending machines are downstairs. I know I don't need anything that's in the vending machines. I had a delicious, abstinent lunch. Why do I feel hungry? What else do I feel?

There is pleasure and satisfaction that the report got completed. It's done — that's a relief — and it seems pretty good to me. I feel that I should celebrate. I deserve a treat. Wanting to reward myself with food is part of the hunger.

Another part is boredom. There isn't anything that interests me very much here in my office right now. The time between this moment and 5:30 p.m. seems very long. When I can't think of something else I want to do, I think about eating. This time I decide to take a break and talk to a co-worker. That should be a pleasant experience — a reward — and should also relieve my feeling of boredom.

8:00 p.m. Taking advantage of the summer evening daylight hours, I have finally started the pruning and weeding that my front yard has needed for weeks. I ate dinner two hours ago and I've been working for an hour when the thought crosses my mind that something to eat would be nice. I'm tired of pruning and weeding, but there's more to do, and I keep at it until 8:30, when it's too dark to continue.

I'm drinking water in the kitchen, and I'm thinking about food. I'd really like something, something soft and filling. Why? I know if I eat a little I will probably binge. That's my pattern. I cannot safely snack.

I manage to get myself out of the kitchen, since that's a dangerous place for me to be. How do I feel? Tired. Very tired. The craving for food is related to wanting an energy pick-up. I'm not really hungry, but I am tired. I'm also getting in touch with some anger that I was feeling about the yard work. I don't like yard work. I'm not sure why I should resent having to do it since it's my house. I can let it go, hire someone to do it, or do it myself, but overeating is not the answer.

Overeating is not the answer to fatigue, either. Going to bed early makes much more sense. I would not be as tired if I had quit working at eight o'clock instead of pushing on for another half hour. I wanted to finish and have it perfect, but at the same time I was angry at myself for not stopping. Overachievement is exhausting, even if it's just pulling weeds. Instead of compensating with extra food, I do go to bed.

69

7:00 a.m. It's the next day and I'm eating breakfast and I think I need more to eat than I had planned. Why? I'm scheduled to be interviewed this morning, and I'm scared. Performance anxiety, the old Waterloo. Admitting to myself that I'm scared gets rid of the urge to overeat. As for the fear, turning my "performance" and the interview itself over to my Higher Power gives me confidence and makes me less afraid.

9:00 p.m. I get a phone call that I've been waiting for, and I am very happy while the conversation is going on. When it's over, I am suddenly empty, and my first thought is — you guessed it — food! The craving is very strong, and I find myself eating a cold potato. (I think I picked the potato in order to convince myself that I wasn't really eating between meals. Who eats cold potatoes for a snack?)

Why am I suddenly starving and eating a cold potato when I don't even particularly like potatoes? The phone conversation was nice. It would be even nicer to be with the person right now instead of waiting to see him Saturday night. Praise the Lord, I am able to *feel* the connection, not just understand it in my head. My hunger is my need for physical contact. Cold or hot, potatoes won't do. When I am willing to feel what is going on, I stop eating. Neither food nor fantasy can substitute for closeness and intimacy with another human being.

* * * *

I can't tell you how many times I have shut off my feelings with food. The good news is that overeaters don't have to overeat. We can learn to experience our emotions fully, without the anesthetic of too many calories. The Twelve Step program promises us a new way of life. Instead of trying to medicate our emotional aches and pains with food, we can turn them over to the care of a Higher Power. As our relationship with the God of our understanding comes more clearly into focus, we are increasingly less dependent on food to make us feel better.

70

Abstinence promotes and enhances feeling. There is simple joy and a sense of being very much alive when you wake up in the morning free from a food hangover. Overeating squelches our emotions. Are you afraid of what might surface if you didn't attempt to keep your feelings in check with food? That's where the Twelve Steps come in. We can learn to let God remove the anger, the fear, the depression, and the hurt so that they do not overwhelm us.

We hunger to experience life in all of its dimensions. Would you be satisfied in "the seasonless world where you will laugh, but not all of your laughter, and weep, but not all of your tears"?[1] To be alive to joy is, of course, to be also alive to sorrow. "The deeper that sorrow carves into your being, the more joy you can contain."[2] What makes it possible to reach the depths and heights without fear of spinning off into outer space is knowing that God is in charge. We are not alone.

I do believe we are not given more than we can handle. Help is always there for us when we ask for it. What we need to do in order to tap in to the limitless source of strength is acknowledge that we can't manage our lives in a satisfactory way by ourselves. Step One, we admit we are powerless. Step Two, we come to believe in a power greater than ourselves. Step Three, we turn our will and our lives over to God's care. Now we are anchored. Paradoxically, surrender makes us strong.

Now we are free to feel whatever comes up, because we have decided to go along with God's plan rather than concocting our own. We have the other nine Steps to guide our growth and keep us on track. If sadness is the order of the day for today, then so be it. We will learn, and we will grow, and there will be more room in our hearts for laughter tomorrow (or maybe even later today).

When we're not obsessed with food, we can get involved in the immediacy of life and be aware of all sorts of things we missed when we were overeating. Abstinence from overeating prompts us to turn to other people to satisfy our hunger for fun, companionship, understanding, and support. We stop shopping for substitutes in the grocery store and begin to find ways of experiencing the real thing. Scary. Risky. Yes. It's also exciting, rewarding, and satisfying. We can start by making new friends in an O.A. group, and who knows where the path will lead? If we believe our Higher Power knows, all we need to be able to see is the next Step.

The path of being willing to feel is a fascinating one, full of insight and surprises. I didn't know how much I missed my mother and father until I stopped simulating their presence with food. I didn't know hurt goes away faster if one is willing to feel it, perhaps shed some tears, and let it pass, instead of spending huge amounts of energy denying it. I'm learning I can say no and watch a relationship deepen instead of disappear. I'm learning I can like myself even though I'm not perfect. I'm learning that letting down my guard and telling it like it is brings others closer rather than pushing them away.

Taking life straight is more fun than being in a food fog. I like myself better. I'm much more "present" with other people and with myself, too. Many of the negative feelings I had when I was bingeing were related to the past. Now, thanks to Steps Four through Nine, most of that dismal residue has disappeared or been washed away. I am free to live and feel in the present, taking each day as a gift from my Higher Power.

How do you feel? Are you willing to continue the adventure of listening to your hunger and discovering what your feelings really are? It's not something we do once and for all, but an ongoing process. When you feel hungry and it's not mealtime, ask yourself what the real issue is. Before you eat, write about it or talk about it. How do you feel right now?

Before, we never had enough.

NINE

The Wisdom of the Body

It has always been with us. Without the wisdom of the body, none of us would have survived. Our bodies possess knowledge that is more immediate than the knowledge of our minds. "Trust your instincts" is usually good advice.

All of us have the ability to know when our bodies need to be nourished, what kind of food we need, and how much. As babies, we all probably start out with this instinctive knowledge about our physical need for food, but somewhere along the line some of us lose it.

Just where and how the loss occurs may be difficult to pinpoint, and the reasons may be debatable. As overeaters, we may blame heredity for dealing out too many fat cells, mother for overfeeding us, an adolescent emotional trauma, frustrations in the present, anxieties about the future, or numerous other factors. Whatever the reasons we cite — past, present, future, physical, emotional, spiritual — what we want to do is recapture our instinctive ability to know what we need and to act on that knowledge.

Most of us know in our heads what we need for good nutrition, but if our natural hunger signals have become distorted through days, weeks, months, and years of overeating, our bodies may not know. Overeating is a very powerful habit which becomes intertwined with a host of different feelings and activities. Our bodies get accustomed to overeating, so they send out signals for food when they don't really need it. The signals are all tangled up with emotions and expectations which have little to do with nutritional requirements.

How do we get back to the wisdom of the body? It's there, if we can break through the distortions and false hunger cues.

Since eating is a habit, our bodies can be retrained to know what they need, when they need it, and how much is enough. If overeating has made our natural instincts unreliable and inflated our appetites out of proportion, we can use external guidelines and controls in order to reestablish the internal ones we have lost. The O.A. program has many tools we need: abstinence and a sponsor help us make our eating pattern healthy and sane. Repeating the healthy pattern one day at a time restores the natural wisdom of the body and guides our appetite back to normal.

We feel so much better physically (emotionally and spiritually, too) when we're eating what our bodies need and not stuffing them with too much and/or the wrong kind of food. Switching from an overload of fats and refined carbohydrates to the right amount and type of nutrients makes an enormous difference in both energy level and emotional outlook. When I was consuming ice cream by the half-gallon, I did not have a lot of energy or emotional stability. Now my body, soul, and psyche thank me twenty-four hours a day because I am concentrating on whole grains, vegetables, fruits, low-fat dairy products, fish, and chicken.

Listen to your hunger. In order to hear the healthy, legitimate hunger of our bodies, we have to filter out the emotional cravings that we misidentify as physical hunger for food. We also have to get off the roller coaster of stuffing and starving.

Overeating means we're out of touch with our bodies' real needs. How does this happen? Many of us, particularly those of us who are female, have been brainwashed by society's overemphasis on how we look and how thin we should be. "Thin is in." "You can never be too rich or too thin." This is the message that continually bombards us through the media and among our peers. Dieting is a national obsession. We restrict our intake severely to try to reach the promised land of slenderness. Our bodies rebel, and we binge. Back and forth. Up and down the scale. In the process, our natural hunger cues are obliterated.

My first diet coincided with my first secret, closet-eating sessions. This was really no coincidence, since dieting and closet-eating go hand in hand. I didn't like the way I looked, and I wanted a fast change. Didn't we all want to lose the weight in a hurry so we could get off the diet? My first diet was crazy. I can remember days of eating nothing but grapefruit, spinach, and hard-boiled eggs. I can also remember skipping lunch except for a dish of ice cream in the school cafeteria and then going home at three in the afternoon and eating everything I could find that was sweet. I alternately binged and dieted my way through high school, college, jobs, marriage, and motherhood. Not very wise, and not very effective.

It's amazing how much sharper my sensations are when I eat three moderate meals each day. For me, abstinence is the key which unlocks my body's wisdom. When I am abstinent, I like my body. I accept its size and shape. I enjoy moving it. New worlds open. I love the sense of well-being and satisfaction that comes from physical exercise, sexual pleasure, standing tall, and breathing deeply.

I'm learning to tune in to the signals my body sends. I find I am hungry for the foods that supply me with the nutrients I need; whole grain bread satisfies me in a way that cookies never did. When I eat slowly and pay attention to inner signals, it is possible for my brain to know when my body has had enough. A balanced, moderate meal will satisfy my physical hunger. Not all the food in the county will fill my emotional and spiritual needs.

I'm learning that regular exercise makes my body feel good. I used to come home from work feeling tired and

77

thinking food was what I needed immediately. I've discovered that a brisk, thirty minute walk not only refreshes me but keeps my appetite at a reasonable level. How about that? Formerly, most of the walking I did was back and forth between the refrigerator and wherever I happened to be in the house.

As long as I am abstinent and do not take that first compulsive bite, I have freedom of choice. I can choose what I will eat. I can choose what I will do and how I will respond to other people. If abstinence goes, so does my ability to choose, since I slip back into the trap of compulsion and self-hate.

My body knows what it needs. It often knows, before my mind does, whether or not I'm in the right place. I get signals of feeling physically comfortable or uncomfortable. Sometimes when my body tells me I'm uncomfortable and in the wrong place, my mind will give me all sorts of reasons for not moving. Behind many of the reasons is apprehension about change.

My body knows when it is in a slippery place — for instance, the wrong section of the grocery store or with the wrong person. Paying attention to these signals and moving when I need to avoids much grief and pain.

How do you feel about your body? It is where you live. Do you take time to listen to the signals it gives you? Do you know what it needs to function well? Do you know when it needs rest? Play? Movement? Sex? Food? A hug? Do you accept what you can't change about your body? Do you aim for the courage to change what you can and the wisdom to know the difference?

We are each a totality of body, mind, heart, and spirit. Though we make artificial separations and divisions for the purpose of describing and analyzing, what we want to achieve is wholeness and unity — smooth functioning of all the parts together. Hunger prompts us to go in search of what we need to keep the totality alive and well. We may not always find what we think we want, but the longer we work the Twelve Step program, the more we seem to get what we need. As we continue to grow spiritually and emotionally, we also refine our ability to understand and act on the wisdom of the body.

We are learning to hunger for spirituality.

TEN

Daily Bread

As long as we are alive, we will not cease to be hungry. There is no finish line. We never reach a state of complete satiation except perhaps when we die. With understanding, hunger can serve as a barometer which measures our general state of health and well-being.

The questions to ask yourself are, "What am I hungering for? What is my hunger really about?" You have a craving, a feeling of emptiness. What will satisfy it? Maybe you used to think chocolate was the answer, but it didn't do the job. Your craving is an indication that you need something, but what? What is your hunger barometer telling you?

The first possibility is that you have a genuine, legitimate need for food, the right kind in the right amounts. When you were small, other people were responsible to see that you got what you needed to eat; now you're on your own. If you don't know what you need to be your most healthy and attractive self, consult a doctor or a nutritionist. Once you know what your body requires to function at its best, use the information to form a daily food plan that works for you.

A second possibility is that your body needs something other than food. Does it need physical activity? Rest? Sensual pleasure? Don't use the excuse of not having enough time. All of us have twenty-four hours in every day, and if we set priorities and use the time creatively, we can do what we really want to do. Physical activity might be as simple as running in place or jumping rope or bending and stretching for fifteen minutes. Rest might mean a twenty-minute nap or foregoing a television program so you get to bed an hour earlier. Sensual pleasure might be a hot bath or looking at a sunset.

Maybe the hunger is not a physical one. Maybe your craving arises from an emotional need. Are you lonely? Would the food you think you want be a substitute for the human warmth and companionship you need? How can you get in touch with other people on a meaningful level so you won't suffer from loneliness? (To be alone is not necessarily to be lonely. If we like ourselves, we can enjoy the times when we are alone.) If loneliness is behind your hunger, pick up the telephone before you take the first compulsive bite. Hug a family member or a friend. Join a club.

Are you angry? Are you afraid? Are you bored? Are you depressed? Are you low on self-esteem? Will extra food make the bad feelings go away for more than a few minutes? Are those few moments of relief worth the subsequent remorse? Talk about the anger and the fear. Use your O.A. group. Get professional therapy. Do both. Most of us need all the help we can get. Find someone else who needs *your* help. Emotions — positive and negative — will pass. And they will come again. Let's learn to go with the flow and not try to medicate ourselves with food. Let your feelings come alive and vibrate. Give way to laughter and to tears. Open yourself to beauty and new experiences. Take life straight, without a sedative.

One of our deepest hungers is our desire for freedom. The Steps of our program lead us out of the trap of false dependencies into a new kind of relatedness. We learn that our security lies in our relationship to a Higher Power and to each other. Living one day at a time sets us free from past regrets and future worries. The program promises us a new freedom — freedom to become who we are by doing God's will.

Listen to the hunger. How is your spirit today? Is it under-nourished? We need daily bread to feed our spirits as well as our bodies and our emotions. Ten years ago I went to my first O.A. meeting, a small group in a church basement. Since then, neither my attendance at meetings nor my abstinence has continued in a solid, unbroken line, though I can honestly say I have been more on than off in both areas. What has been constant for me during these last ten years is setting aside time for spiritual nourishment at the beginning and end of each day.

The way it works for me is to spend a few minutes when I first wake up in the morning turning the day and my life over to God's care, reading from two meditation books, and tuning in to my center. At night I also spend some time being quiet, often taking an inventory for the day, and seeking to improve my conscious contact with my Higher Power.

This spiritual nurturing has been, I believe, the driving force behind the remarkable changes which I have experienced since joining the program. If you were to ask me what is most important in my life, I would be hard-pressed to choose between abstinence and spiritual growth. For me, they go together. I don't think I can have one without the other.

I believe spiritual growth is what life is ultimately all about. The fruits of the spirit satisfy my deepest hunger. I think inner growth is more exhilarating than any chemical or caloric high, and there is no hangover. There is adventure, and there is peace. There is love for and from my fellow human beings. There is quiet confidence that God is in charge.

I am grateful that my unmanageable hunger led me to the Twelve Step program. Without the pain and chaos of my eating disorder, I don't think I would have surrendered to a Power greater than myself. Skepticism and doubt would have overruled belief, if not for the fact that coming to believe was my only possible way out of pain and despair.

Listen to the hunger. We are all part of a spiritual network, and we need contact with one another to foster and reinforce our inner growth. We hunger to be of service, to feel our lives have meaning and count for something. A truism of our program is that we keep it by giving it away, by sharing it. I hunger to make contact with you, to listen to you, support you, share with you. I need your listening, your support, and your sharing. May God be with us and guide us as together we do what we cannot do alone, as we each discover what it is that we crave and learn what satisfies.

ENDNOTES

Chapter One
[1] *Alcoholics Anonymous* (New York, Alcoholics Anonymous World Services, Inc., 1955), p. 55.

Chapter Two
[1] *Twenty-Four Hours a Day*, Revised Edition (Center City, MN, Hazelden Educational Materials, 1975, order no. 1050), entry for June 24.
[2] The Big Book is *Alcoholics Anonymous*, published by A.A. World Services, Inc., New York. Available through Hazelden Educational Materials, order no. 2020.

Chapter Three
[1] Kahlil Gibran, *The Prophet* (New York, Alfred A. Knopf, 1959), p. 19.

Chapter Six
[1] C.G. Jung, edited by Violet S. de Laszlo, *Psyche & Symbol* (New York, Bollingen Foundation, Inc., 1958. Garden City, New York, Doubleday Anchor Books, Doubleday & Company, Inc.), p. 72.
[2] *For Today* (Torrance, CA, Overeaters Anonymous, Inc., 1982), p. 201.

Chapter Seven
[1] T.S. Eliot, "Little Gidding," *Collected Poems, 1909-1962* (New York, Harcourt Brace Jovanovich, 1963), p. 209.
[2] Lao Tzu, *Tao Te Ching*, Chapter 16.
[3] Holy Bible, Psalm 46, verse 10.
[4] T.S. Eliot, "Ash Wednesday," op. cit., p. 86.

Chapter Eight
[1] Kahlil Gibran, *The Prophet* (New York, Alfred A. Knopf, 1959), p. 12.
[2] Ibid., p. 29.